a lift·the·flap book abo

MW01504846

What do you eat?

Sally Lloyd-Jones and Rick Brown

Zonder**kidz**
The Children's Group of ZondervanPublishingHouse

What do you eat?
Do you
eat bones?

What do you eat?
Do you eat
flowers?

What do you eat?
Do you eat worms?

What do you eat?
Do you eat hay?

What do you eat?
Do you eat grass?

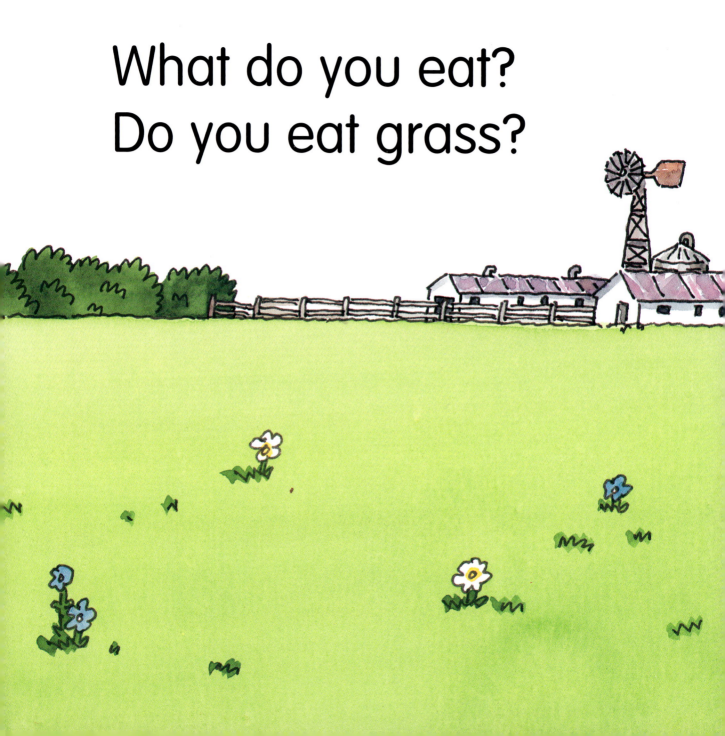

What do you eat?
Do you eat flies?

What do you eat?
Do you eat acorns?

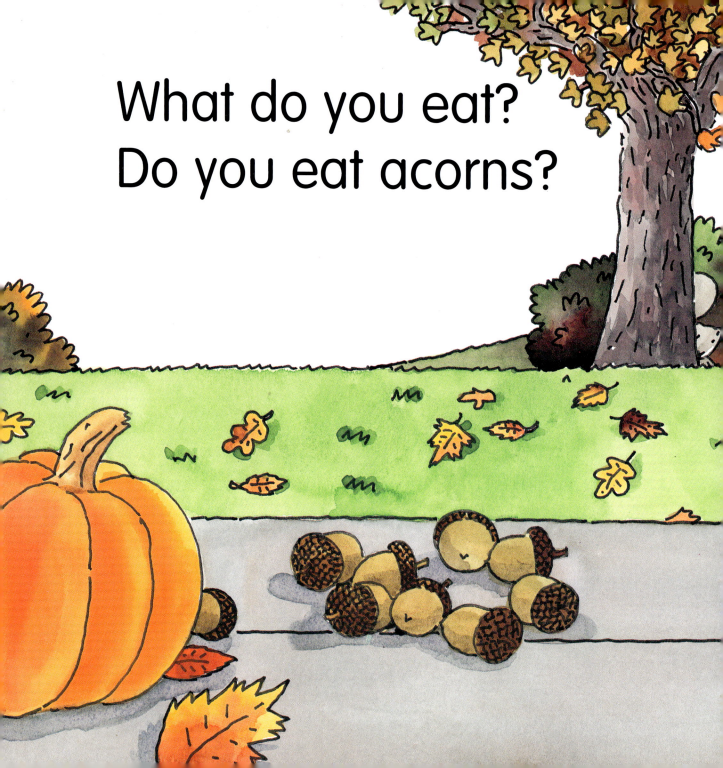

What do you eat?

Jesus said that God loves us like a good daddy. He looks after us. He gives us clothes to wear. He gives us somewhere to live. He gives us food to eat.

from Matthew 6